Fairies and Dragons
Adult Colouring Book

With Artist Lee Pryke

Fairies and Dragons

ISBN: 1522778233
ISBN-13: 9781522778233

DEDICATION

My Grandson, Honour Short; inspired me when he was four years old to start having more fun and playing with art. His framed art hangs on my walls encouraging me to
'let the little girl inside come out to play'
This was the beginning of me drawing and creating art and now comes together in a series of colouring books for others to enjoy.

Fairies and Dragons

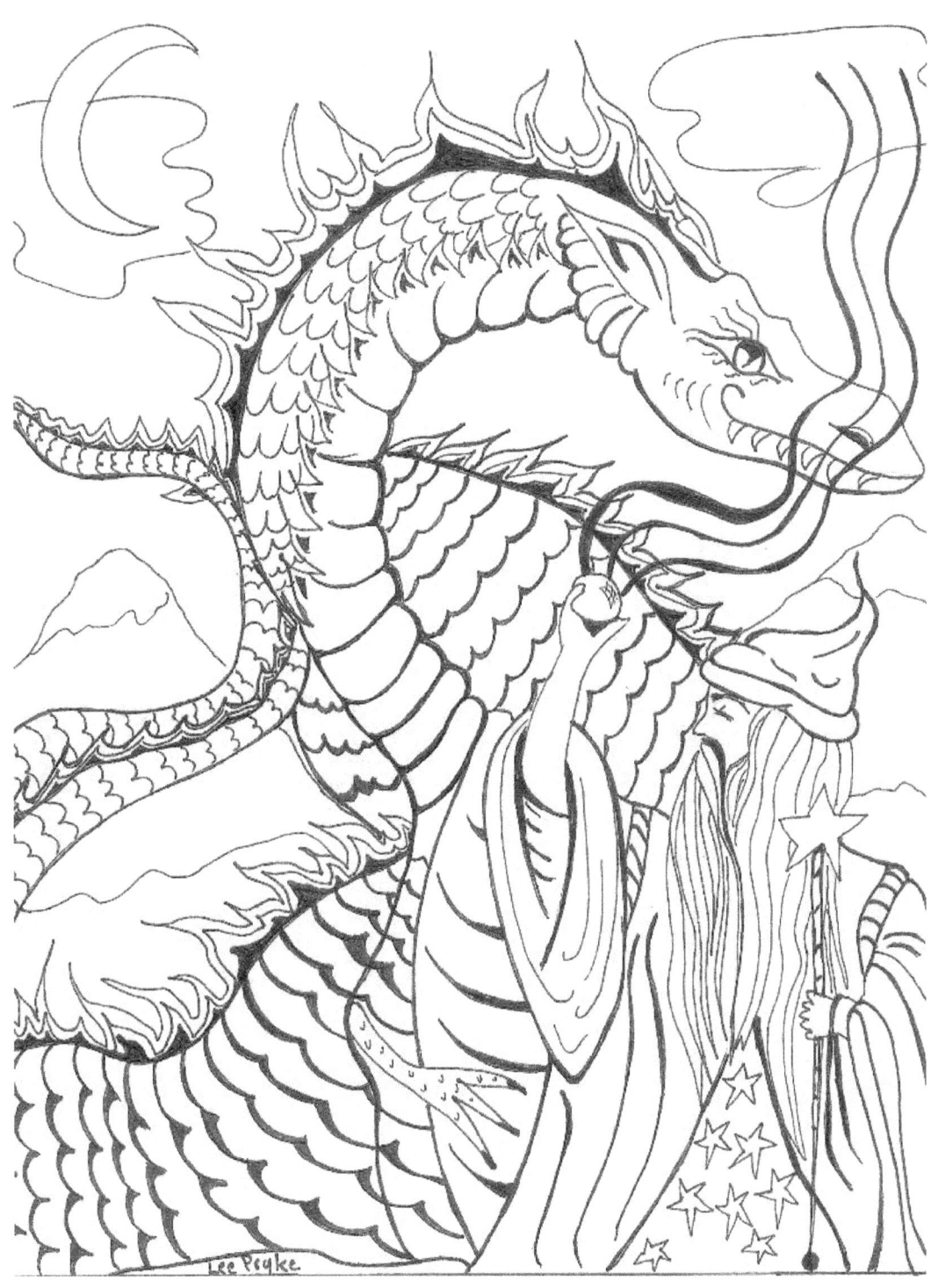

Fairies and Dragons

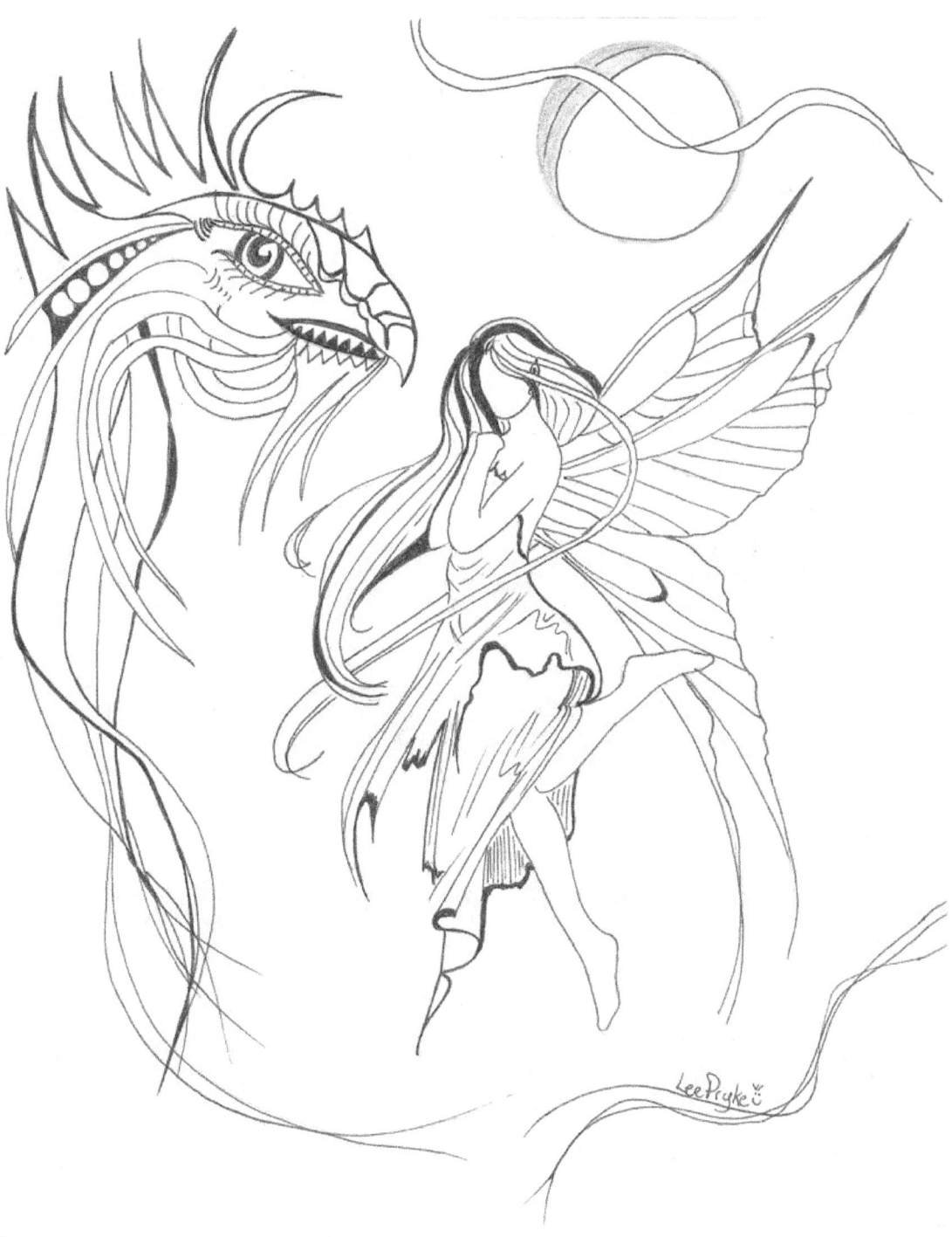

Fairies and Dragons

Fairies and Dragons

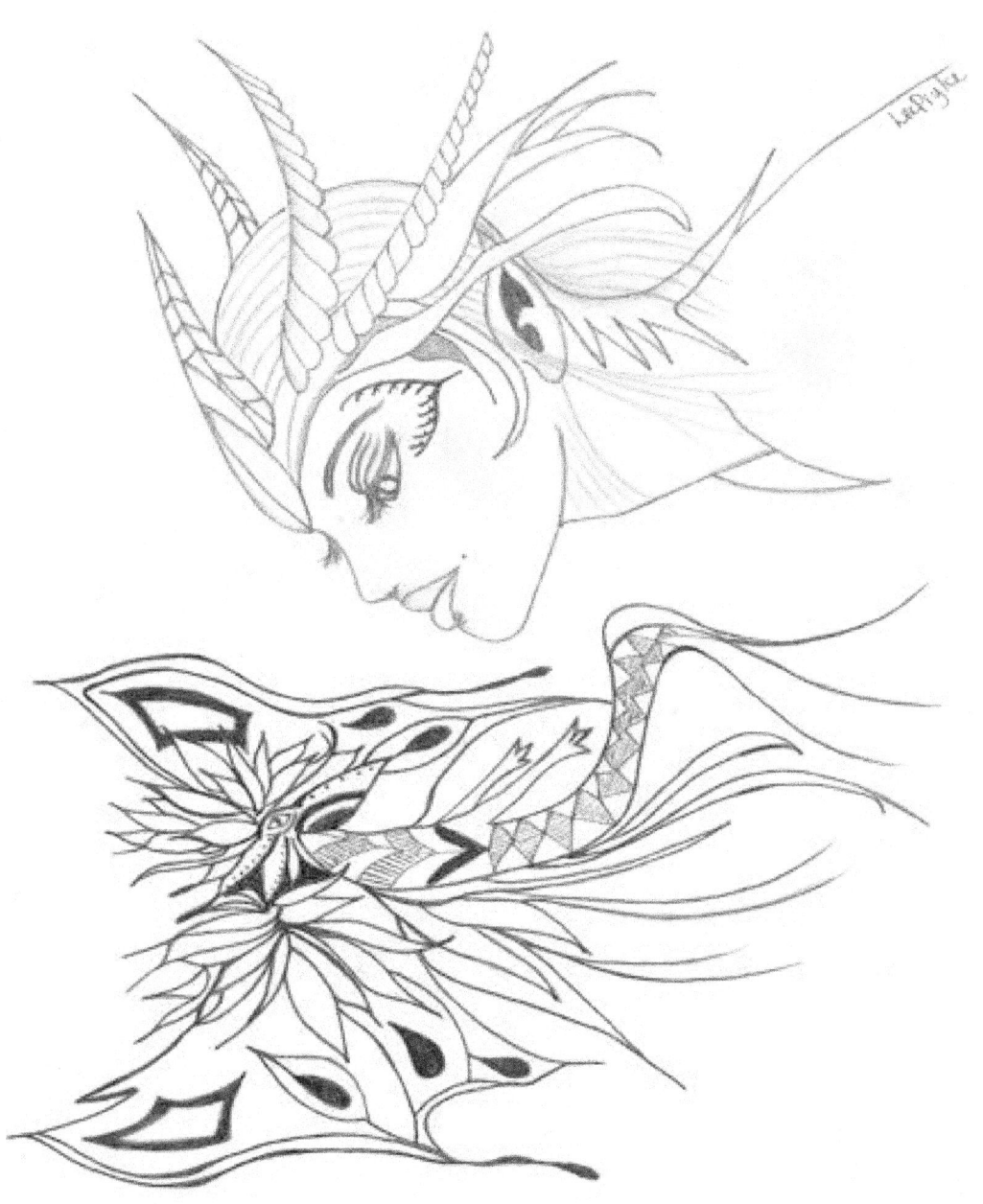

Fairies and Dragons

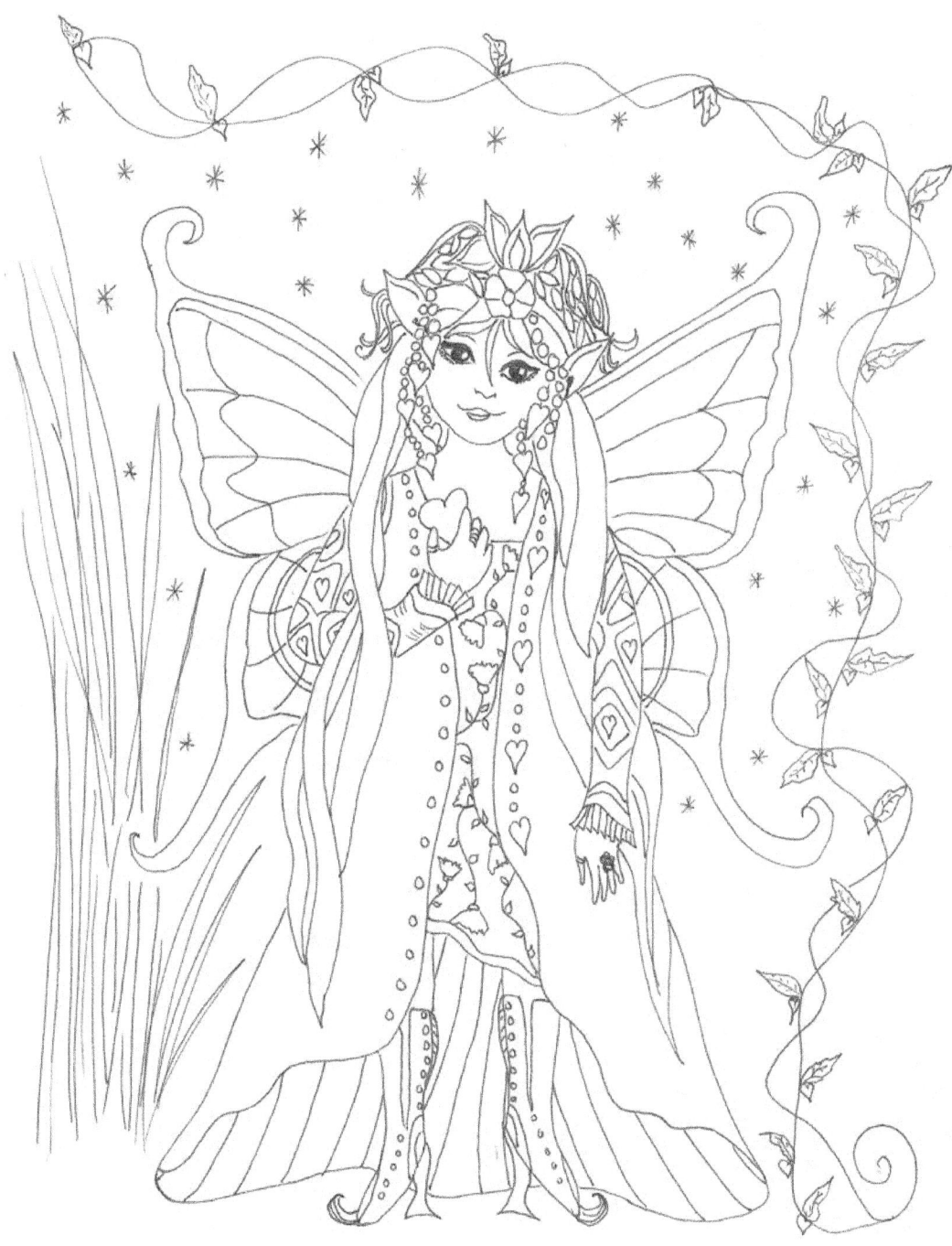

Fairies and Dragons

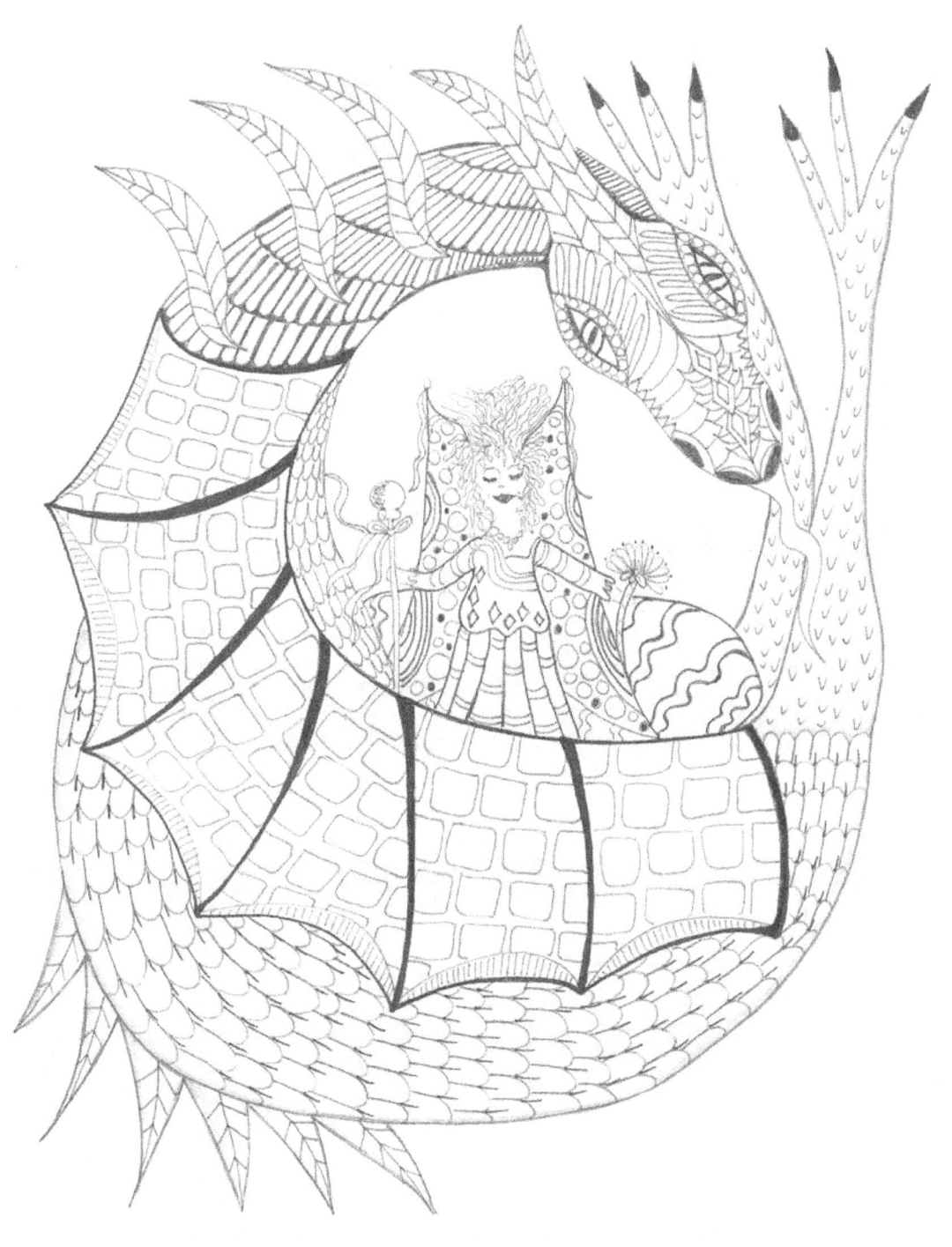

Fairies and Dragons

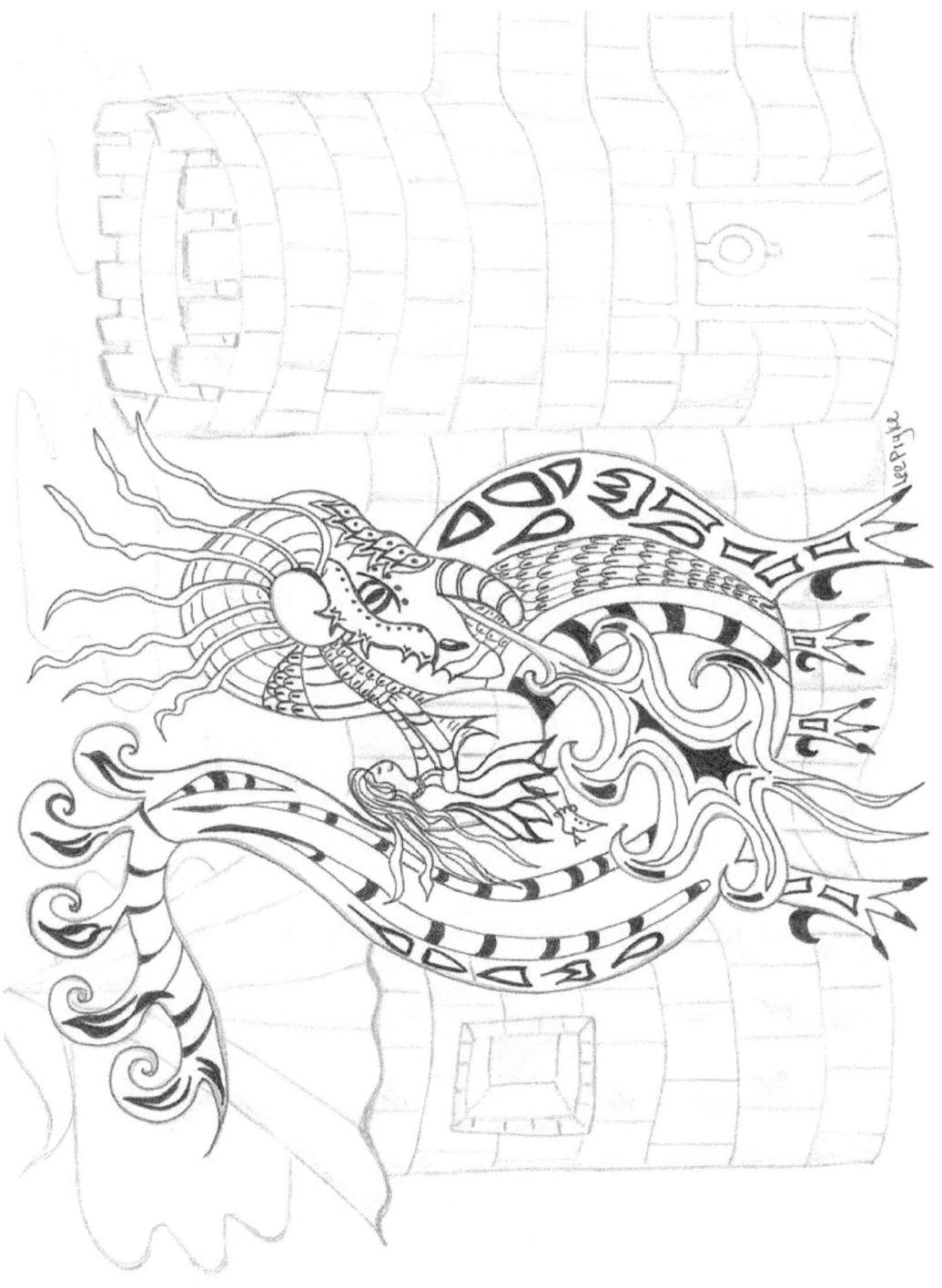

Fairies and Dragons

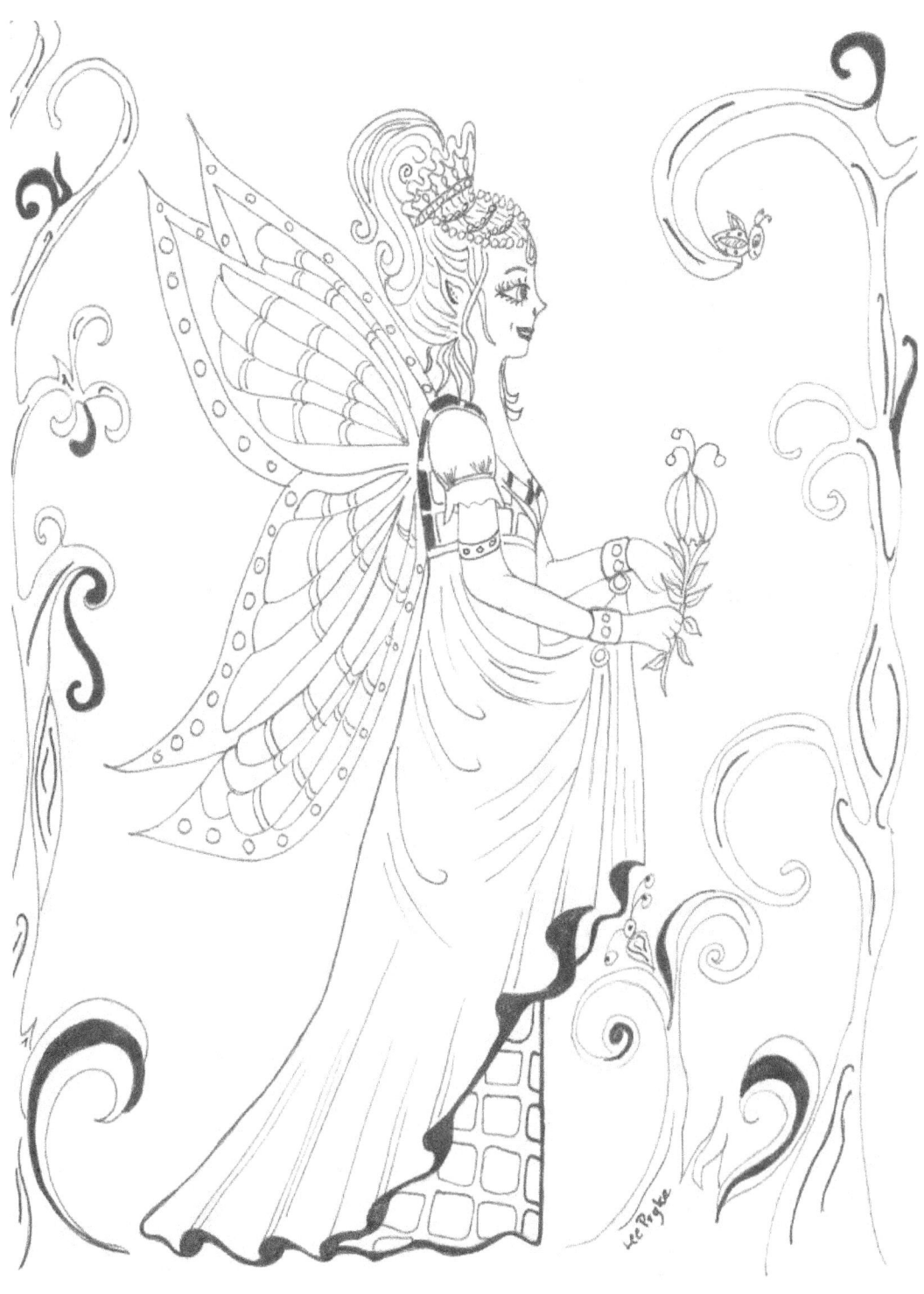

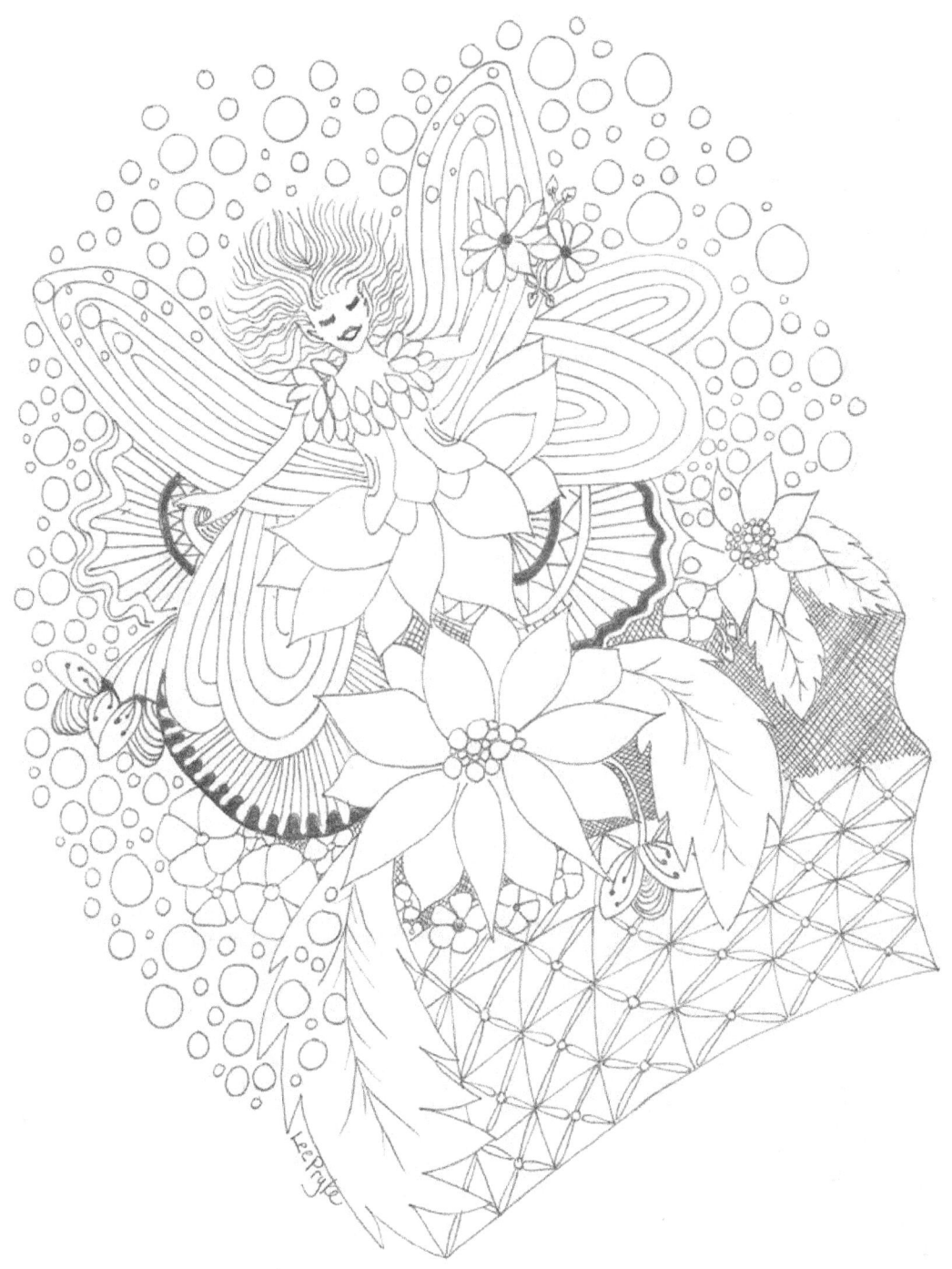

Fairies and Dragons

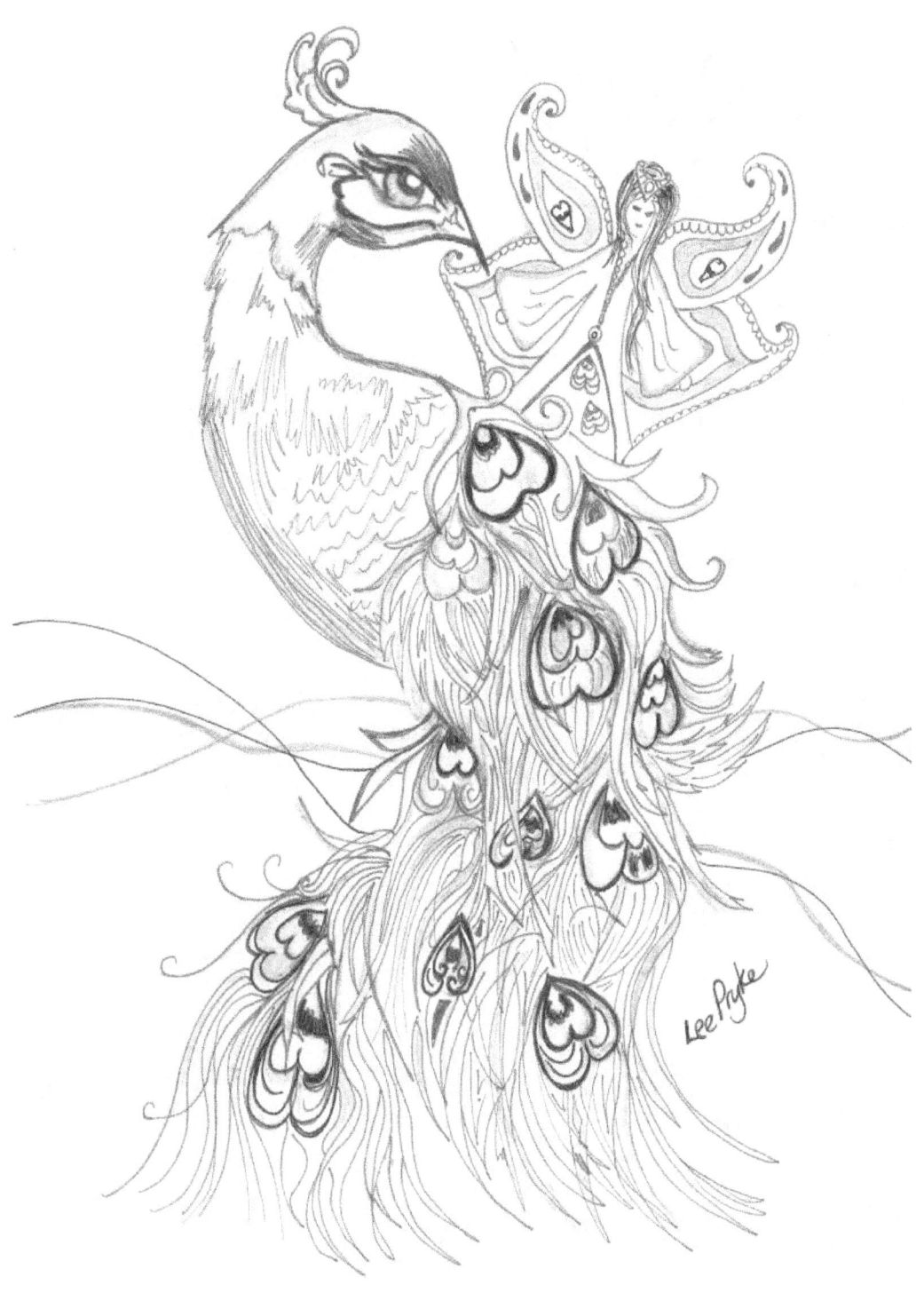

Fairies and Dragons

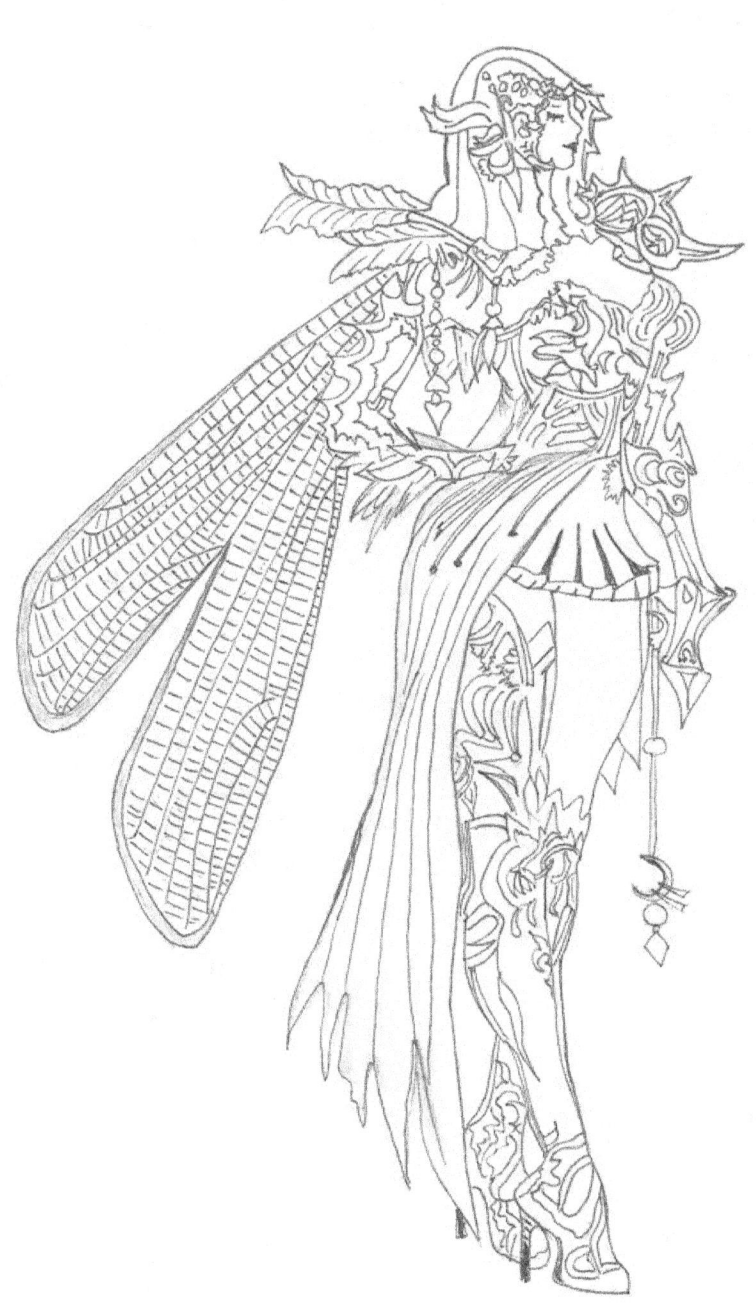

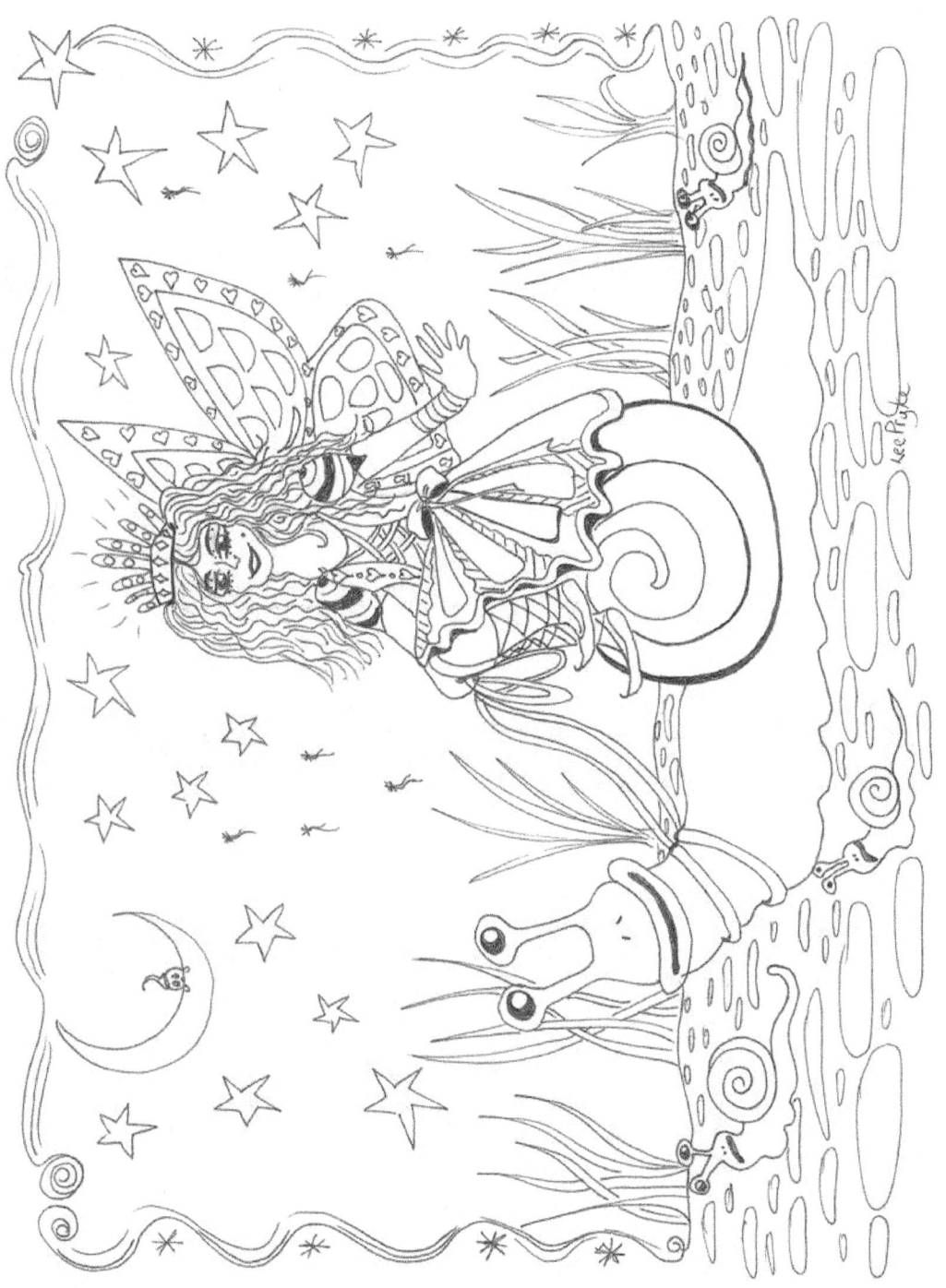

Fairies and Dragons

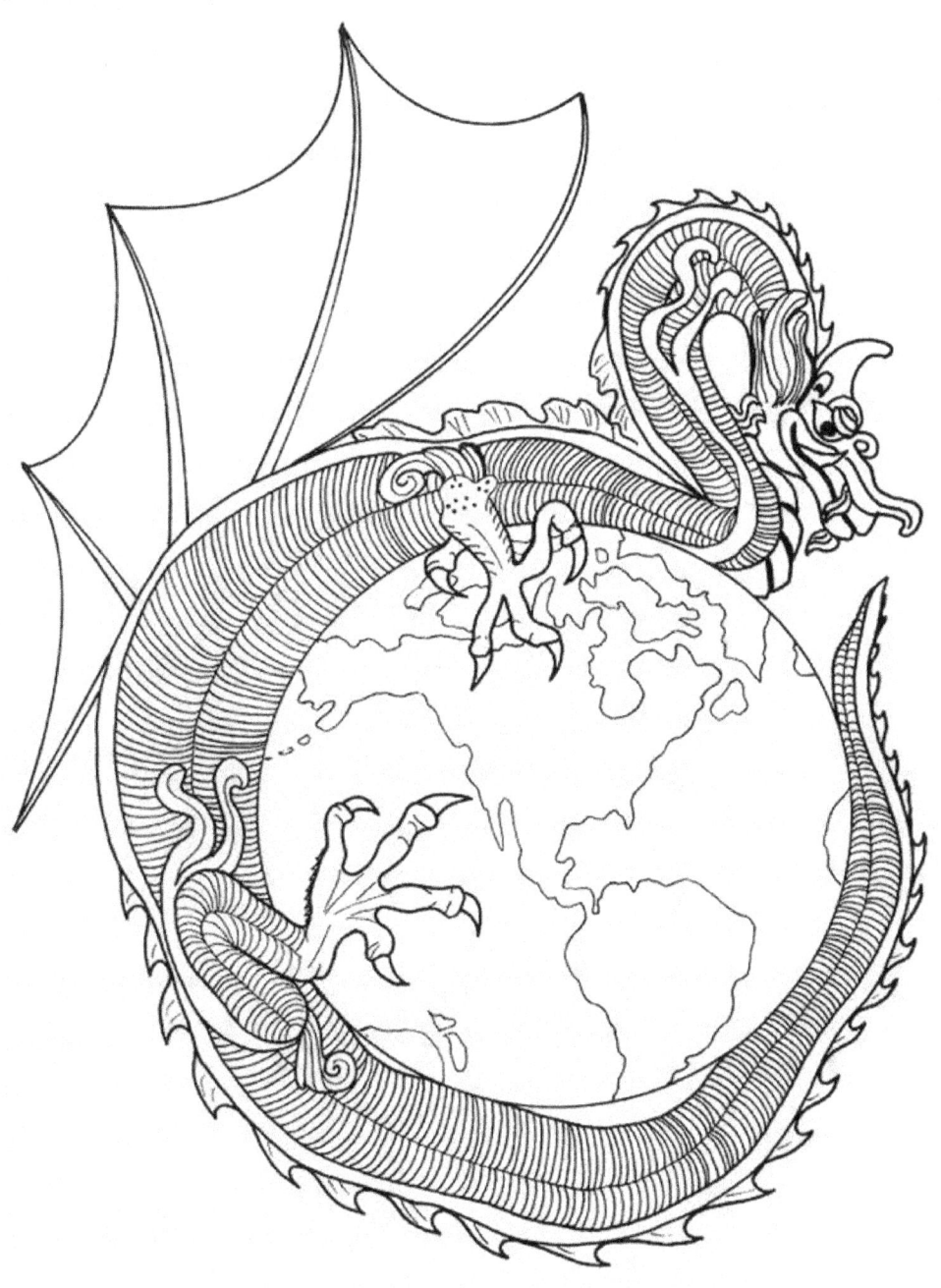

Fairies and Dragons